POWER
IN GOD'S WORD

SUSAN SHERWOOD PARR

Published by

WORD PRODUCTIONS
ALBUQUERQUE, NM USA

Power In God's Word
by Susan Sherwood Parr

Copyright ©2015 by Susan Sherwood Parr
http://www.susanparr.org
http://www.lifetotheworldministries.org

Published by
Word Productions
Albuquerque, NM 87111

Printed in the United States of America.

ISBN 978-0-9909245-9-3

Table of Contents

᷏

1

The Integrity
of God's Word

❦

*I will give you the treasures of darkness
and hidden riches of secret places, that you
may know that I, the LORD, who call you by your
name, am the God of Israel.* Isaiah 45:3

The purpose of this book is twofold:
first, to inspire the reader to a deep
love and respect for the integrity God's
Word; and second, to renew his or her joy
and excitement in the fact that the Bible
contains supernatural power that will
transform all of us. The Word is part of
God Himself, and it reveals His character,
personality, and heart. Together we will
uncover the many treasures found within
the holy Scriptures.

1

Following, are several facts about the Bible that will help to clarify the nature and character of God:

Fact One: God and His Word are one.

In the beginning was the Word, and the Word was with God, and the Word was God. John 1:1

Fact Two: The Word of God was written as men were led by the Holy Spirit, and there were scribes that recorded the words spoken by the prophets (2 Peter 1:21). Baruch wrote the words that God gave to Jeremiah. The epistles were letters that Paul the apostle wrote as he was led by the Holy Spirit:

For prophecy never came by the will of man, but holy men of God spoke as they were moved by the Holy Spirit.
2 Peter 1:21

For this reason we also thank God without ceasing, because when you received the word of God which you heard from us, you welcomed it not as the word of men, but as it is in truth, the word of God, which also effectively works in you who believe.
1 Thessalonians 2:13

2

Fact Three: God's promises are true.
For all the promises of God in Him are Yes, and in Him Amen, to the glory of God through us. 2 Corinthians 1:20

"So shall My word be that goes forth from My mouth; it shall not return to Me void, but it shall accomplish what I please, and it shall prosper in the thing for which I sent it." Isaiah 55:11

Fact Four: We obtain His promises.
Do not become sluggish, but imitate those who through faith and patience inherit the promises. Hebrews 6:12

...By which have been given to us exceedingly great and precious promises, that through these you may be partakers of the divine nature, having escaped the corruption that is in the world through lust. 2 Peter 1:4

Let us hold fast the confession of our hope without wavering, for He who promised is faithful. Hebrews 10:23

Fact Five: God *wants* to fulfill His promises to all who believe.

For everyone who asks receives, and he who seeks finds, and to him who knocks it will be opened. Matthew 7:8; Luke 11:10

Do not fear, little flock, for it is your Father's good pleasure to give you the kingdom. Luke 12:32

If you then, being evil, know how to give good gifts to your children, how much more will your Father who is in heaven give good things to those who ask Him! Matthew 7:11

The Supernatural Power
In the Word

There is supernatural power in the Word of God, which is the Bible. It is neither a "bunch of words" nor just a "historical book."

If Jesus was just "a good man or a prophet," as some religions refer to Him, the Bible would be worth reading. But Christ is God in the flesh, the Son of God, the promised Messiah, and He is God.

The Bible is the only prophetic book with a proven track record of fulfilled prophecies. There are over three hundred fulfilled prophecies in the Bible. There is no other religion that can say this about their writings. We have the proof!

The Bible is the Word of God. Many miracles confirm this, and many lives have been transformed through implementing its principles. It is indeed a precious treasure.

It is the Spirit who gives life; the flesh profits nothing. The words that I speak to you are spirit, and they are life. John 6:63

In the above verse, the word "spirit" means breath, and the word "life" means:

ZOE: (Greek) Life in the absolute sense, life as God has it, that which the Father has in Himself, and which He gave to the Incarnate Son to have in Himself; and the life that He gives He maintains. Definition from *Vine's Expository Dictionary of Biblical Words*

John 6:63 provides biblical evidence that there is supernatural life within God's Word. Is that true? Is there evidence? Many great things have happened in the lives of those who spend time in the Word of God. In the Jesus

Movement, many kids who had been on drugs and whose minds were nearly destroyed found healing in their minds when they read the Bible.

One whose life was dramatically changed during this time was Mike Macintosh, a pastor in southern California. He tells his own story, saying that he was so burnt out on drugs that he even thought part of his brain was gone. Mike came to Jesus Christ and found total healing through Jesus Christ and the Word of God. He now brings the healing found through life in Christ to others.

The healing power in God's Word began long ago. The promise of healing began in the Old Testament:

> *My son, give attention to my words; incline your ear to my sayings. Do not let them depart from your eyes; keep them in the midst of your heart; for they are life to those who find them, and health to all their flesh.* Proverbs 4:20-22

The above scripture is evidence that God's Word is *alive* and has *life and healing within itself.*

The Supernatural Drawing
Power in the Word

We can be drawn to God in a number of ways. We can be drawn by the power of the Holy Spirit and through the hearing of God's Word.

The Scripture contains verses that indicate that God draws people to Himself through the power of the Holy Spirit. What a wonderful thought it is that God has such great love that He would draw us so that we can come close to Him. Here are some scriptures that prove this fact:

> *Blessed is the man You choose, and cause to approach You, that he may dwell in Your courts. We shall be satisfied with the goodness of Your house, of Your holy temple.*
> Psalm 65:4

> *"No one can come to Me unless the Father who sent Me draws him; and I will raise him up at the last day."*
> John 6:44

> *"And this is the will of Him who sent Me, that everyone who sees the Son and believes in Him may have everlasting life; and I will raise him up at the last day."* John 6:40

"All that the Father gives Me will come to Me, and the one who comes to Me I will by no means cast out." John 6:37

Another way through which a person can be drawn to God is through the hearing of the Word of God. It seems so silly, so foolish. Take a look at the following scriptures:

So then faith comes by hearing, and hearing by the word of God. Romans 10:17

For since, in the wisdom of God, the world through wisdom did not know God, it pleased God through the foolishness of the message preached to save those who believe. 1 Corinthians 1:21

For the message of the cross is foolishness to those who are per-ishing, but to us who are being saved it is the power of God. 1 Corinthians 1:18

Therefore He who supplies the Spirit to you and works miracles among you, does He do it by the works of the law, or by the hearing of faith? Galatians 3:5 (also 3:2)

And when the Sabbath had come, He began to teach in the synagogue. And many hearing Him were astonished, saying, "Where did this Man get these things? And what wisdom is this which is given to Him, that such mighty works are performed by His hands!" Mark 6:2

Born Again Through the Word?

Can anyone be "born again," receive "salvation," or "be redeemed" though His Word? Most definitely, the answer is "YES!" The redemptive work of Christ on the cross enables us to receive the wonderful gift of being redeemed or born again. Through Christ's sacrifice of Himself, we can now receive God's life. Whatever your terminology, you can be born again (become a spiritual new creation in Christ) through His Word:

Having been born again, not of corruptible seed but incorruptible, through the word of God, which lives and abides forever. 1 Peter 1:23

How Can You Have This Miracle?

This miracle can take place in anyone's life. If you are a born again Christian, the Holy Spirit dwells in you. If you are not, repeat this prayer:

> *Dear God, thank You for sending Your Son, Jesus Christ, to die in my place for my sins, and for raising Him from the dead. I ask You to forgive me of all of my sins and to come into my heart right now. I ask You to be the Lord and Savior of my life. Take control of my life, and make me into the person You want me to be. Amen.*

If you weren't born again, you are now. The Holy Spirit indwells the Christian. God will do a beautiful work in your life. There is nothing too hard for God (Genesis 18:14). Remember, let God and His Word do a mighty work in your life. If you've thought of giving up...don't! Let Christ live His life through you. Turn it all over to Jesus, and remember, there is nothing too hard for the Lord.

3

CHAPTER

The Word Is Working
Within You!

❦

How can our lives be changed by God's
Word? Power lies within the Word of
God itself and in its Author. The proof not
only lies within the Scriptures, but is
evident in the lives of people's lives with
whom it comes in contact.

How Does God's Word Affect Our Lives?

When a person accepts Jesus Christ as
his or her Lord and Savior, the human spirit
is made alive. The person is truly changed.

In 2 Corinthians 5:17 we read: "Therefore, if anyone is in Christ, he is a new
creation: old things have passed away;
behold, all things have become new."

13

If you will look up the meaning of "creation" in *Vine's Expository Dictionary of New Testament Words*, you will find that it means the following:

Creation as a noun, 2937, ktisis: *Primarily "the act of creating," or "the creative act in process," as in 2 Corinthians 5:17 "new creation."*

If any man is in Christ, he is a new creation. Think about that: a total transformation and creation has taken place in the spirit realm. That is a stimulating thought. God is alive today, works miracles today, and works in the human spirit today.

Saved Through the Word

The Bible says that man comes to Him through the foolishness of preaching (1 Corinthians 1:21). The fact that a man came and died for our sins is not something we hear every day, and it seems strange to the natural man or woman. Even the term "saved" seems odd to us who have not grown up hearing it with an understanding of what it means. Yet there is supernatural power within God's words, whether written or spoken; there is enough power to cause transformation and miracles to occur.

This miracle of spiritual life through the redemption that is in Jesus Christ is what the human race needs. It is indeed a miracle.

We Are His Workmanship

The Bible says that we are God's handiwork, or "workmanship."

For we are His workmanship, created in Christ Jesus for good works, which God prepared beforehand that we should walk in them. Ephesians 2:10

We are God's handiwork, or "workmanship." The Greek word for "workmanship" is *poivhma*. Here is the definition from *Strong's New Testament Greek Lexicon:*

That which has been made

1. a work

   a. of the works of God as creator

The Word Producing Fruit IN You!

God is at work within you, producing Holy Spirit fruit. Isn't that a comforting thought?

> ...Because of the hope which is laid up for you in heaven, of which you heard before in the word of the truth of the gospel, which has come to you, as it has also in all the world, and is bringing forth fruit, as it is also among you since the day you heard and knew the grace of God in truth.

Colossians 1:5-6

First Peter 1:23 teaches us that God's Word is an incorruptible seed. It says that this seed of God's Word lives, abides, remains, and stays *forever*. What a thought!

Not only is the Holy Spirit at work within our lives, but His Word is at work within you. One of my favorite verses that proves this is found in 1 Thessalonians 2:13:

> For this reason we also thank God without ceasing, because when you received the word of God which you heard from us, you welcomed it not

16

*as the word of men, but as it is in
truth, the word of God, which also
effectively works in you who
believe.*

This powerful, living Word has the
power to raise us to life in Christ. It is an
incorruptible seed that lives inside of us
forever. This great seed of the almighty
God "effectively works" in us! That's
good news. There is hope for us all.

There is power within the Gospel of
Christ to bring us to Jesus Christ to be
born again. Then we can enjoy the wonderful fellowship with God and share in
His promises made to us in His Word.

*But we all, with unveiled face,
beholding as in a mirror the glory
of the Lord, are being transformed
into the same image from glory to
glory, just as by the Spirit of the
Lord.* 2 Corinthians 3:18

Digging for Treasure

A re there treasures in the Holy scriptures? Yes, there are. After we take a
look at the meaning of the word"treasure,"
we will tell you how to find your own treasure in God and His Word. Is the word "treasure" mentioned in the Bible?

> *I will give you the treasures of dark-*
> *ness and hidden riches of secret*
> *places, that you may know that I, the*
> *Lord, who call you by your name,*
> *am the God of Israel.* Isaiah 45:3

After reviewing four commentaries on
Isaiah 45:3, I found that none of them
defined the "treasures in secret places."

What was the Holy Spirit referring to in this promise? This was a prophecy about the future of Israel.

The word "treasure" is used in a large number of verses and in many different contexts in the Bible. Its meaning is not hidden, but rather it is used in the simple definition of the word:

> **Treasure:** \Treas-ure\, v. t. (imp. & p. p. Treasured; p. pr. & vb. n. Treasuring.) To collect and deposit, as money or other valuable things, for future use; to lay up; to hoard; usually with up; as, to treasure up gold. (Webster's Revised Unabridged Dictionary, © 1996, 1998 MICRA, Inc.)

> **Treasure:** n 1: accumulated wealth in the form of money or jewels etc.; "the pirates hid their treasure on a small island in the West Indies" (syn: hoarded wealth) 2: something highly prized for its beauty or perfection (syn: gem) 3: any possession that is highly valued by its owner; "the children returned from the seashore with their shells and other treasures" 4: a collection of precious things; "the trunk held all her

meager treasures" v 1: hold dear; "I treasure these old photographs" (syn: prize, value, appreciate) 2: be fond of; be attached to (syn: care for, cherish, hold dear) (WordNet ® 1.6, © 1997 Princeton University)

For the purposes of discovering God's heart in its usage, let's look at the many varieties of the word's interpretation. First, we'll look at what man has thought that the word "treasure" means in Isaiah 43:5, and then we will look at the scriptural references that contain the word.

What Does Man Say?

From man, I have heard the following descriptions of what "treasure" might mean:

1. **Treasure could be** the gems and oil of the earth that have blessed mankind.

2. **Treasure could be** the archaeological finds that confirm God's holy Word.

3. **Treasure could be** actual buried treasure that God caused people to find.

What Does the Bible Say?

The Word of God mentions the word "pearls" in the scripture in Matthew 7:6 that instructs us:

> *Do not give what is holy to dogs; nor cast your pearls before swine, lest they trample them under their feet, and turn and tear you in pieces.*

Here, "pearls" are referring to the holy things that God has given to us. These things can include what we have to say about God, His Word, or what He has done in our lives.

The Pearl of Great Price

The Bible speaks of the kingdom of heaven as a treasure and as a precious pearl in Matthew 13:44-46:

> *Again, the kingdom of heaven is like treasure hid in a field, which a man found and hid; and for joy over it he goes and sells all that he has and buys that field.*

> *Again, the kingdom of heaven is like a merchant seeking beautiful*

pearls, who, when he had found one
pearl of great price, went and sold all
that he had and bought it.

Other References to "Treasure"

The following scriptures contain the
word "treasure." Through them, we can see
that the Lord is referring to many treasures,
including spiritual treasures.

The LORD will open to you His good
treasure, the heavens, to give the
rain to your land in its season, and to
bless all the work of your hand. You
shall lend to many nations, but you
shall not borrow. Deuteronomy 28:12

With Your hand from men, O Lord,
from men of the world who have
their portion in this life, and whose
belly You fill with Your hidden treas-
ure. They are satisfied with children,
and leave the rest of their possession
for their babes. Psalm 17:14

There is desirable treasure, and oil in
the dwelling of the wise, but a foolish
man squanders it. Proverbs 21:20

Wisdom and knowledge will be the stability of your times, and the strength of salvation; the fear of the L*ORD* *is His treasure.* Isaiah 33:6

For where your treasure is, there your heart will be also. Matthew 6:21

Jesus said to him, "If you want to be perfect, go, sell what you have and give to the poor, and you will have treasure in heaven; and come, follow Me." Matthew 19:21

Sell what you have and give alms; provide yourselves money bags which do not grow old, a treasure in the heavens that does not fail, where no thief approaches nor moth destroys. Luke 12:33

So when Jesus heard these things, He said to him, "You still lack one thing. Sell all that you have and distribute to the poor, and you will have treasure in heaven; and come, follow Me." Luke 18:22

But we have this treasure in earthen vessels, that the excellence of the power may be of God and not of us. 2 Corinthians 4:7

*I rejoice at Your word as one who
finds great treasure.* Psalm 119:162

Finding Your Treasures

In the previous verse, God refers to the
the Holy Spirit's indwelling as a "treasure."
Indeed, it is. Here are a few things we
know are *spiritual* treasures:

- Enjoying a relationship with God
- Holy Spirit revelation of Scripture
- God the Father, Son, and Holy Spirit
- Redemption in Christ
- Forgiveness of sins
- Access to the grace of God
- His Word
- Promises of God
- Gifts of the Holy Spirit
- His provision
- Miracles
- Deliverance
- Angels that fight for and protect us
- Eternal life in heaven

These are only a few, but think of it:
God is our most precious treasure. The
very words of God are a treasure! All that
He is and does is wonderful. He is truly
the almighty God.

It's MY Turn

Jesus Visits My Life

❧

God began to move in my life when I was a young, married mother. His most precious treasure was about to reveal Himself to me in a new way.

My mother had us regularly attending a denominational Christian church. I was taught purity and to avoid all sin (and what sin was) at a very young age. God even worked in my life at that young age. The problem was, He was "way up there in the sky" to me, and I could *only* pray to Him in that way.

I was later taught in private school to ask the Holy Spirit to enlighten me, so I asked for the Holy Spirit's inspiration for my tests in school. That was good enough for me. At about the age of twelve, I found a "holy card" with Mark 11:24 on it. It said that if I asked anything in Jesus' name and believed that I received it, I could have it.

I felt I had found a gold mine. Well, that was that. I started praying. At that time, my prayers were silly kid things. I had no idea of the power of God, or dimension of God though Christ, that could be mine.

At age nineteen, the hand of God was drawing me to something I didn't have. I couldn't put my finger on it, but I was spiritually hungry and desirous of the supernatural in my life. I couldn't find it. I began reading books on the supernatural like *Cybernetics, The Power in the Mind,* and anything I could find that had to do with power beyond the natural.

Guidepost's magazine ended up at our house a couple of years later. It was addressed to "resident," and that was ME. I was so inspired by these stories of actual miracles. I had been taught to give every day to God, which I was doing, but the desire for Him to own me and have my life more than I had was growing within me.

A young woman who was selling cosmetics with me was a born-again Christian
(as a mother, I sold cosmetics or vitamins
to supplement our income). I was in a con-
versation with this girl who seemed *too
enthused* about God—her approach was
foreign to me.

She asked me, "Can I mail something
to you? It really helped me." I was angry at
her in my heart but had a second thought:
"In the spirit of ecumenism" I would let
her mail this to me. "Okay," I said. The letter arrived. This was the first time in my
life that I let a letter lay on the shelf for
four days before opening it. Finally, I
opened it, and inside of it was Campus
Crusade for Christ's *Four Spiritual Laws*
booklet.

"What is this? ...oh brother," I thought. I
opened it and skeptically and critically
read through it. I read the prayer to ask
Jesus Christ into my heart with arrogance
and skepticism. *Something* (I now know it
was the Holy Spirit) made me read the
prayer once again...this time with feeling.
"Where did my nice attitude and feeling
come from that caused me to read it
again?" I wondered.

I later realized that I had experienced the truth in the scripture that tells us that our redemption through Christ is a gift of God, of grace, not works, lest any man should boast (Titus 3:5).

My Visit to Albuquerque

The next thing that happened to me is that I visited my family, then living in Albuquerque, New Mexico. Hippies and guru-seeking people were everywhere. One night at my mother's house my brother had one of his new friends over. He was one of these seekers. He said to me, "Oh, God is inside of each of us. We all have God." I thought, "Oh no...this is too much." Now I needed some answers for myself.

"God, You Show Me!"

I knew what I had to do. I walked outside one evening, and just as I did as a twelve-year-old, I began talking to God, whom I had always termed as "my real Father." "God," I began, "I know You exist and that You are a Supreme Being, or God. YOU show me if Jesus is real and if and how significant this is to me. I don't want to base my entire life on something someone else told me to believe. YOU show me if this stuff about Jesus and if Jesus is real."

That was it! I had done it. I left my request with the God of the universe there. I was going to wait for a real answer. I knew that I would know if God Himself revealed anything to me.

Campus Crusade for Christ

When I returned to Georgia, I was invited to a Campus Crusade for Christ nondenominational Bible study, which I felt I could attend *only* because it was inside of a neighborhood house, showing no partiality to a particular denomination. I began there, to learn how to "turn things over to the Lord." That's where I met Donna MaGill. She became my friend, and she and her husband were actually like spiritual parents to me. Donna and I had prayed the same prayer to God, "that He show us His will for our lives." She had made the same mistakes I had made. I was running around trying to find it. It was through Donna and the Crusade for Christ Bible study that I first learned how to be led by the Holy Spirit. In the meantime I had found a book, if you can believe this, on Christian yoga.

The Meditation Experiment

As I mentioned earlier, I had gotten my hands on everything that had to do with the supernatural, etc., and had begun to try meditation. I decided one night to set a candle in front of me on a table and to look through it to a glass (my china cabinet) and just stare at the glass, meditating. "Okay...now what was going to happen." I just sat there on my knees. Then I actually saw something. I saw the picture in the glass of people in a circle, wearing brightly colored clothing, dancing around and waving their arms wildly. Over to the right side of the picture I saw a shadow of what looked like Jesus Christ.

I thought about this. I remembered a time when I visited my aunt at age fifteen. She had all sorts of books in her closet upstairs on Zaoism, Taoism, and there was one on witchcraft. I had picked up the one on witchcraft and randomly opened it and looked through it. It described a scene exactly like what I had seen on the glass of my china cabinet...except that Jesus Christ was missing from the picture. I didn't realize until months later that the Holy Spirit was showing me that what I was doing in this time of meditation was witch-craft... and that Jesus Christ was in the shadows. This type of meditation was not of God.

God Showed Me!

About six months after my prayer for God to show me if Jesus was really God and how significant it was for my life, it became crystal clear.

God did it! He did it through events that were not coincidental events, scriptures I would randomly open to, words people would say (who didn't know what I was asking of God), and undeniable supernatural manifestations of the Holy Spirit that began happening in my life. What happened next was the most exciting of all.

6

The Jesus Movement:

Miracles Everywhere

❦

The Jesus Movement was a great move of the Holy Spirit that appeared on the scene in the 1960s-1970s. I heard the following stories and many others that took place during Jesus Movement:

Nuns at at a convent were having prayer time...suddenly, the Holy Spirit came upon them and they began to lift their hands and praise the Lord; they began to speak in tongues and prophecy; to glorify God.

By most accounts, the Jesus People Movement began in 1967 with the opening of a small storefront evangelical mission called the Living Room in San Francisco's Haight Ashbury district. Though other missionary-type organizations had preceded them in the area, this was the first one run solely by street Christians. (oneway.org/jesusmovement/-index.html)

Something changed my life radically during the Jesus Movement. I saw young people out walking on the streets of the town I was living in carrying Bibles. They actually looked like Jesus' disciples.

God was moving all over the world, and the news of it spread to all.

I wanted more fervor. I had been going to Bible studies and seeing God actually lead me, but I was hungry for more of God. Soon I faced an onslaught of temptation. I prayed, "God, isn't there something more? I don't know if I can make it."

One day Donna invited me: "Susan, we've been going to these really great prayer meetings in this psychologist's basement in Conyers, Georgia. Do you want to come with us?

She tried to prepare me: "They speak in tongues and raise their hands and praise the Lord."

That was it! I had only heard the first half of the description, but I had heard *enough.* "Spoke in tongues? Wasn't that the *devil's* stuff? What on earth were they into?" I approached her with my questions.

Donna, with her unending patience and wisdom told me of John Sherrill's book, *They Speak with Other Tongues,* and of how this scholar set out to disprove the validity of speaking in tongues as a gift of the Holy Spirit. "Why don't you read the book, Susan? Just ask the Lord to show you if it is true or not." There she went again with that same trite phrase that ended all of my questions: "Just ask the Lord to show you." Why was it that it always worked? I got a the book and read it. I then asked God to show me for myself.

I still did not know what I thought, even though, amazingly enough to me, there were even scriptures that mentioned tongues. It amazed me. I had never heard anything about this being in the Bible. But yes, there were the scriptures in my Bible, along with "Jesus Christ, the same yesterday, today, and forever."

I mustered up some courage, and at the spur of the moment, I decided to go to one of these prayer meetings.

The Psychologist's Basement

That Friday night, I walked into the psychologist's basement. There, seated all around the floor, were young people from about sixteen to twenty-four years of age. The floor was covered with people talking about Jesus.

The psychologist was a man of medium height with a nonconservative (of course) look about him, a little beard, and John Lennon glasses. This was great! I took a seat. Donna and John were already there.

The prayer meeting began. We started to sing some songs. I was not familiar with any of them. Today, I still remember: "Silver and gold have I none, but such as I have give I thee. In the name of Jesus Christ of Nazareth, rise up and walk." Even the songs were filled with the miracle-working power of Jesus Christ.

The room grew quiet and the psychologist instructed us all to say or whisper, "Thank you, Jesus" and "I love you, Jesus."

Though skeptical, I thought, "Even I can do this."

He began prayer, "Lord, You promised that where two or more are gathered in Your name, there You are in the midst of them. We claim that promise right now!"

Suddenly, the entire room filled with a heavy manifest presence of the Lord. It felt like liquid love. That's the only way I can describe it. Why had I never felt anything like this before? Where had I been?

I nudged the girl sitting on the floor next to me. "Do you feel that?" I asked.

"Feel what?" she answered.

"That heaviness, that feeling in the room," I said.

She got a heavenly look on her face and answered me by saying, "Oh...I always do."

Always do? Always do...what? I could not believe it. What was all this? Where had I been? What was going on?

That evening I left with many questions. Of course, Donna said, "Just put it all on the shelf, Susan, and say, 'Lord, I don't understand this. You show me if this is all real or not.'" What a way to get off the hook! But you know, it always worked! It still does. I continued to seek the Lord about all of these new things.

I went back the next Friday night. A man walked up to me and gave me a copy of *In His Steps*. He said, "I don't know why, but I just feel led to give you this book." What he didn't know was that there was a girl in the book who fit my description and who hadn't given her singing voice to the Lord.

That girl was me. I sang professionally for a time, and I grew up performing, entering talent contests, etc., and the only religious expression of music I had seen was through church choirs. I was delighted that God wanted all of me and my gifts—I gave my musical gifts to God.

Next, a girl came up to me and said, "The Lord has shown me that He has a *special gift of peace* for you. Just claim it."

Just before I went to the prayer meeting that night, an unusual thing had happened to me. I had been in a marriage with someone who was abusive. He was becoming increasingly violent. He went on a rampage that day, and just before the prayer meeting, he shook his fist at me in a rage.

Instead of being afraid, I felt an uncanny peace all over me. It was amazing. It was so much peace that I thanked God for this unusual covering of peace. Then I went to the prayer meeting, and the girl told me of the gift of God I had just experienced. It *was* the truth!

What a prayer meeting that was! Needless to say, I was hungry for what else the Lord might do in my life.

Just the Beginning

That was another new beginning for my life. I continued to hear of marvelous things the Lord was doing. I heard of people being delivered from drugs with no withdrawals following, of appearances of Jesus Christ, of physical healings...the list was unending.

I later went back to the Friday night prayer meeting and received the baptism in the Holy Spirit. It was as though a big spiritual door opened for me. Just the thought that God actually had plans for my life thrilled me.

In those days, people passed books around, sharing the exciting things God was doing, like no other time I've seen since. People were starving to hear about a supernatural God who was alive. Jesus was and is alive and well and doing miracles. This was in the 70s. It was known by all as "The Jesus Movement."

It was like in the book of Acts. God was doing something. There are a variety of doctrines. There a lot of views as to what is going on "right now." This was a time and a season. Historically, God has poured out His Spirit. If you study its history, you will see it.

We do need to be careful to keep sound doctrine and not assume anything.

The Word clearly says "not all speak with tongues." When God pours out His Spirit, He manifests himself in the way He wants for that time.

This outpouring was called "the Jesus Movement," and was happening all over the world in the late 60s and in the 70s. The greatest thing is that it started the study of His Word and regular prayer in my life!

7

You Are What You Eat:
Physically and Spiritually
❧

What effect can the Word of God have on your life? What will it "produce" on the inside of you? Believe me, there is supernatural power within the Word of God. It can and will produce inside of you.

First, I want you to remember that within the Word of God is His breath, the very life of God:

> It is the Spirit who gives life; the flesh profits nothing. The words that I speak to you are spirit, and they are life. John 6:63

The words from God are spirit and they are life.

We Are Triune Beings

We are a three-part, or triune, being. We have a spirit, a soul, and a body. We are more than just flesh and blood; there is more to a human's life than just a body. The words in 1 Thessalonians 5:23 depict this for us:

> *Now may the God of peace Himself sanctify you completely; and may your whole spirit, soul, and body be preserved blameless at the coming of our Lord Jesus Christ.*

Natural Food

Natural man is fed and sustained by natural food. You have probably heard the expression "You are what you eat." There have been studies to indicate that your body and your mind react to whatever you take in: The body responds to the type of food you eat, and the mind and your actions are affected by the media and type of life you expose yourself to. Another expression is "Garbage in, garbage out." Eat junk food, and your health will decline. Eat healthily, exercise, and get proper rest, and your body

will positively react as well. You will be
healthy and strong and probably feel
better than if you didn't.

Spiritual Food

The spirit is fed and sustained by the
spiritual food of God's Word. The following scriptures will help you to see how it
works:

> But He answered and said, "It is
> written, 'Man shall not live by
> bread alone, but by every word
> that proceeds from the mouth of
> God.'" Matthew 4:4

> As newborn babes, desire the pure
> milk of the word, that you may
> grow thereby. 1 Peter 2:2

> Therefore lay aside all filthiness
> and overflow of wickedness, and
> receive with meekness the
> implanted word, which is able to
> save your souls. James 1:21

God's Word Producing...

What are some other specific things
that the Word of God will produce in
your life?

The Word Brings Healing

Have you ever walked through a greenhouse? Have you ever noticed how great the plants look? Why do they look so good? It's because they are planted in healthy soil with the right nutrients in it. The temperature of the greenhouse is perfect for the plants. The plants are given just the right amount of water. When we buy these plants, if we don't tend to them in exactly the same way, they began to look a little shabby.

God's Word Changes My Thoughts

Once, while I was going through a trial in my life, God gave me a little nudge on the inside of my heart. It was as simple as: "Everything is going to be all right." The silent "voice" of God filled me with enough hope and faith to be totally relieved and made me know that I would definitely make it through the trial. It was faith received from God Himself. The "word" was from the Lord, and there was power in it. This blessing will happen to us all as we continue our relationship with Christ. He loves us all.

46

The Secret Formula

There is no secret formula. There is, however, dynamite power in God. He is limitless and powerful, and nothing is too hard for Him. The power is in Him; the power is in trusting in His promises. He means what He says and He never lies.

There is an awesome story in the Old Testament that I want to share with you. It will leave no doubt regarding the power of God to move on your behalf. It is the story of God's prophet, God's people who trusted in God, and what happened to those with whom they were at war. Check this out:

> Now the king of Syria was making war against Israel; and he consulted with his servants, saying, "My camp will be in such and such a place." And the man of God sent to the king of Israel, saying, "Beware that you do not pass this place, for the Syrians are coming down there." Then the king of Israel sent someone to the place of which the man of God had told him. Thus he warned him, and he was watchful there, not just once or twice.

Therefore the heart of the king of
Syria was greatly troubled by this
thing; and he called his servants
and said to them, "Will you not
show me which of us is for the
king of Israel?"

And one of his servants said,
"None, my lord, O king; but Elisha,
the prophet who is in Israel, tells
the king of Israel the words that
you speak in your bedroom." So
he said, "Go and see where he is,
that I may send and get him."

And it was told him, saying, "Surely
he is in Dothan."

Therefore he sent horses and chariots and a great army there, and
they came by night and surrounded the city. And when the servant
of the man of God arose early and
went out, there was an army, sur-
rounding the city with horses and
chariots. And his servant said to
him, "Alas, my master! What shall
we do?"

So he answered, "Do not fear, for
those who are with us are more

*than those who are with them." And
Elisha prayed, and said, "LORD, I pray,
open his eyes that he may see." Then
the LORD opened the eyes of the
young man, and he saw. And behold,
the mountain was full of horses and
chariots of fire all around Elisha. So
when the Syrians came down to him,
Elisha prayed to the LORD, and said,
"Strike this people, I pray, with blind-
ness." And He struck them with blind-
ness according to the word of Elisha.*

*Now Elisha said to them, "This is not
the way, nor is this the city. Follow
me, and I will bring you to the man
whom you seek." But he led them to
Samaria.*

*So it was, when they had come to
Samaria, that Elisha said, "LORD, open
the eyes of these men, that they may
see." And the LORD opened their eyes,
and they saw; and there they were,
inside Samaria!* 2 Kings 6:8–20

This is such a great story. Did you know
that nowhere in the Bible does it say that
God won't or can't do these same things
for us today?

The Lord never said we would live without trouble or without spiritual battles, but He did say He would give us the victory and that He would lead us in triumph:

Now thanks be to God who always leads us in triumph in Christ, and through us diffuses the fragrance of His knowledge in every place. 2 Corinthians 2:14

Yet in all these things we are more than conquerors through Him who loved us. Romans 8:37

But thanks be to God, who gives us the victory through our Lord Jesus Christ. 1 Corinthians 15:57

Making It Work:
Create a Word Atmosphere

❧

L ike a plant, if you are surrounded with the right conditions, etc., you will thrive. When you surround yourself with a Holy Spirit and Word of God atmosphere, it's like a spiritual greenhouse—and from this atmosphere, a Holy Spirit and godly fruit is produced in your life. Your whole life can change.

A Word Atmosphere

How do you surround yourself with a Word atmosphere? Here are a few tips:

1. Faithfully attend a praying, power-of-God-believing church.

2. Be certain that your church believes in the inerrancy of the Word of God.

3. Spend time with God on a regular basis.

4. Read the Bible; if you prefer, listen to Bible recordings or teachings.

5. Fill your life with the things of God.

"Rest" on the Promises?

God also backs up His written word and promises by the power of the Holy Spirit. Believe me, if God said it, it will happen. When you pray and rest on His promises for your answer, He will definitely answer. God responds quickly when we ask Him to help us grow spiritually. It is His will.

Prayer is a wonderful means of communicating with our God. We spend time with Him, sharing our deepest feelings with Him. We worship Him, telling Him how much we love Him and how thankful we are for His kindness and goodness. We also share our deepest needs and concerns with him.

If you don't spend any devotional or quiet time with God, it is time to start. If you need to, you can begin with ten minutes twice a day and work your way up. Just do whatever you can do. Just start!

How do you "rest" on God's promises? The following points will help you understand what resting on His promises means.

1. His promises are true.

2. When we pray about forgiving others, to receive grace, for help in trials, and for many other things, we are praying according to God's will.

3. When we pray scripturally, asking the Father in Jesus' name, as is taught in the Bible, we can rest and place our faith and trust in the truth of His Word.

   He finishes the scripture by saying: "I will do it"; "you shall have it"; "everyone that asks receives"; "ask and you shall receive that your joy may be full"; and on and on.

4. Rest all of your hopes in God. You can rest; you can trust in God. You can trust Him to keep His promises.

5. Next, begin to thank Him and praise Him for what He is doing (according to His will).

Your Miracle of Transformation

Surround yourself with a Word atmosphere, and you will see your life change. Even Jesus said that they that abide in Him will bear fruit. Here are some of the noticeable changes you will experience:

- You will develop and grow spiritually as the Word of God is developed in you and as you are fed the Word of God.

- You will be able to recognize God speaking to you in the Word of God. His Word is His voice. He never says anything that is not in line with His written word.

- You'll find yourself thinking and feeling differently. You will be changing from glory to glory (2 Corinthians 3:18).

- You will be able to discern the voice of God as you develop and grow spiritually. You will learn that you don't always have to jump if you "think" something is from the Lord. You will begin to take time to weigh what you think and feel with what the Bible says. You will be able to test it.

- You grow spiritually. Many are healed mentally, spiritually, and emotionally through the Word of God. Healing will spring forth from your life.

   My son, give attention to my words; incline your ear to my sayings. Do not let them depart from your eyes; keep them in the midst of your heart; for they are life to those who find them, and health to all their flesh. Proverbs 4:20-22

- You will grow to worship the God of the Bible.

The Promise of a New Nature

   ...By which have been given to us exceedingly great and precious promises, that through these you may be partakers of the divine nature, having escaped the corruption that is in the world through lust. 2 Peter 1:4

We can be transformed through faith in the promises of God written for us long ago and recorded in His Word, and as we do so we are made partakers of HIS

nature. The Holy Spirit lives within us.
Note that the Holy Spirit is God—that's
His nature. What promises say that we can
have His nature? Take a look at Ezekiel
36:26-27:

> *I will give you a new heart and put a
> new spirit within you; I will take the
> heart of stone out of your flesh and
> give you a heart of flesh. I will put
> My Spirit within you and cause you
> to walk in My statutes, and you will
> keep My judgments and do them.*

What more could any of us want?
He will put His Spirit within us and
cause us to walk in His statutes.
Don't say, "I can't do it. I just can't
make it." God can do it. It is HE who
works within you to will and do what
He wants.

*For it is God who works in you both
to will and to do for His good pleasure.* Philippians 2:13

*...And what is the exceeding great-
ness of His power toward us who
believe, according to the working of
His mighty power.* Ephesians 1:19

God Is My Treasure

I Am His

℀

God in our lives is indeed our greatest treasure. Do you realize that you are a treasure to Him? Look at these scriptures:

> *Then those who feared the LORD spoke to one another, and the LORD listened and heard them; so a book of remembrance was written before Him for those who fear the LORD and who meditate on His name.*

> *"They shall be Mine," says the LORD of hosts, "On the day that I make them My jewels. And I will spare them as a man spares his own son who serves him."* Malachi 3:16–17

"Now therefore, if you will indeed obey My voice and keep My covenant, then you shall be a special treasure to Me above all people; for all the earth is Mine." Exodus 19:5

For you are a holy people to the LORD your God; the LORD your God has chosen you to be a people for Himself, a special treasure above all the peoples on the face of the earth. Deuteronomy 7:6

For the LORD has chosen Jacob for Himself, Israel for His special treasure. Psalm 135:4

For the last part of our study, I want you to meditate on the goodness of God and His love. Think about the good things: the power of God; His abiding presence: His wonderful love.

Write your thoughts of Him. Write your thankfulness to Him. Write your meditations of Him and of His Word. God is a good God!

God, My Treasure